FEVERS OF THE MIND POETRY DIGEST ISSUE 3

THE DARKNESS AND THE LIGHT

INTRODUCTION:

We entered the Autumn.

The season of Halloween and fallen leaves.   The cooling in the air. We feel the beginnings of early darkness.

It all feels dark for months upon month, until the warm air and sunlight arrives again.

When we feel the darkness, the depression, the anxiety.

What is there? Is it there? Does it touch? Do you have the bravery to overcome?

Challenges and fears.   That snow melts rather easily when you breathe upon it.

We have to pull at the cracks to look for that light on the other side of this wall.

The Darkness & the Light

Table of Contents

© David L O'Nan

The Ride © John Everex

They look like my sons, but they're not. I pretend they're driving me to town as usual, but the radio news verifies my suspicion: there's no way Carl would listen to that man and not shout obscenities. At eighty-two, I'm old enough to know leukemia ain't gonna' kill me, despite it running wild through my withered body. No, it'll be my heart, as it was for my pa and his before him. I've done well getting this far - it's further than they did. The engine shifts as we drop a gear, approaching the turnpike, the freeway continuing on toward the southern cities. We're headed toward the open space of the mountains as I thought. I try to examine the boys in the front, but my eyes haven't worked in years. They're soft focus, which is romantic and cosy they say, but I can't see shit.

I left my glasses at my place.

Utopia Mansions it's called - my place - a bit like a cheap motel, but full of old shufflers and nosers. I'd wanted a beachside residence with a view of the sea, but I got rooms smelling of old man's piss and cleaning chemicals. My home isn't much different from the hospital mom pushed me out into. Liz is laughing at me, wherever she is - she died ten years ago of lung cancer, a lifetime of smoking and a slow death being strangled by the shit inside her lungs - but at least she doesn't have to live at Utopia Mansions.

The car slows further, the mountains still a purple bruise. We pass a rest area, a camper van spilling people from inside. Kids. A dog. We used to do that as a family. "We used to do that," I say, my voice croaking. They ignore me and I feel like shouting. But I remind myself, they are not my sons and I'm not going to give them any satisfaction. I stare out of the window as mute as the dead, trying to get my brain in gear. I used to be top notch, to matter, until the agency made cuts and our department was no longer needed. Severance they called it, a pension

and a long slide into retirement.

I look for indications of who they are - the similarities with Carl and John are uncanny -

they dress the same. Similar haircuts. Of an age. New clothes. Both of them. That's the thing, my

sons never went for fashion; thrift store or second-hand was their style. These two are dressed

up to look like my sons, but wearing new clothes, judging by the creases in the never-worn-

before shirt. The way fake Carl holds the wheel too; his hands are uptight and professional, not

the slouch that Carl takes, one hand always itching to hold a cigarette like his mum.

And he's not smoking.

And they still say nothing.

As we pull into a petrol station, I see the restrooms,

knowing this might be my only chance.

What If © Ann Hultberg

Suffering in 99 degree heat, and by that time wearing sweat soaked clothes, my husband, daughter, and I finished hauling her many bags and boxes up three flights of stairs to her tiny dorm room. It was a Saturday afternoon and we were dropping our daughter off for her first semester of college. After spending several hours getting her settled, our daughter was anxious for us to leave. She had already spotted another girl her 5 foot ten height and wanted to know where she had bought her jeans. Ready to join in the activities for incoming freshmen, she wanted us gone. Folding and refolding her clothes in her dresser drawers, I was in no hurry to leave her. On her desk I laid out her stationary and book of stamps; though she might not write letters home, I would be writing to her every day.

What she didn't know was that once I hit these narrow dorm hallways, an old feeling returned - my first semester I-hate-it-here college memories hit me like it was I starting my college career all over again. Panicked feelings overcame me, and I wanted to pack my daughter back in the carand take her home away from here. I didn't want her to be fearful, alone, and anxious as I was at her age when I left home for college.

My panic attacks started at Girl Scout camp. We eight-year-olds slept outside in raised tents and

rose each morning to a bugle call. A week-long Separation from family made me anxious. So, I started to squint -left eye, right eye, back and forth marching tics, left, left, left right left. Next blinking ensued between squinting tics. I would pucker my lips and pull back into a grin. These exhausting yet necessary facial movements required concentration--the pattern had to be followed-- a little girl's toolbox for dealing with separation, with anxiety. The camp counselor talked to my mom about my mannerisms on our last day as we girls performed skits for our parents. My mother told me later that she was shocked and a bit embarrassed by such abnormal facial movements.

She worried this would continue but all such antics stopped once I returned back home again.

But ten years later, when I left for college, the anxiety returned in a

different form: eye tics were replaced by hair pulling.

I stepped out of my daughter's dorm room and into her hallway- so narrow -only one person could pass through at a time. The low ceilings reminded me of Lego blocks, shaped that way to cushion sounds from any noisy upstairs neighbors. As my daughter milled among the other girls in the hall, I looked for an escape window. The dichotomy of our situations, apparent only to me, brought me back to my first days at college.

Grab a strand and pull. Grab a strand. Pull. Again and again.

Short, brown hairs collected on my desk. A nest- like pile of worries scattered over a composition notebook, blue Corona typewriter, and 16 LB bond typing paper. The scalp endured this pain without complaint. My bald spot enlarged each night.

Next, I attacked both eyebrows. Pinch a strand and yank. Smooth the brow over and pinch again and yank one fine sliver of brown at a time. Blow them off the fingertip, again and again. My once thickly shaped eyebrows became a thin crescent of bristles.

Trichotillomania - a type of impulse control disorder, pulling hair as a way to soothe oneself. But it didn't always work. Nightly Anxiety grabbed for my attention. I hyperventilated. In the dorm hallway I gulped for air that didn't seem to be there. Rapid breaths came; I forced myself to inhale and exhale to slow my heartbeat. Back in my room, a small black and white TV calmed me--Saturday Night Live brought me back to reality vs my rampant imagination. My TV was my best friend.

I feared that:

- I would stop breathing,

- My parents would soon die and who would raise the younger siblings?

-I would be alone.

I was only seventeen and missed my house noise, the familiar. I wasn't used to the quietness, the open space, and the uncontrolled thoughts that veered toward the negative and tragic. I turned into a hypochondriac, unhappy, not adjusting like other freshmen seemed to be.

My mother and grandmother wrote to me often as did my younger siblings. I daily checked my mailbox for letters from home, which got me through those initial months. I felt connected and could visualize all the activities happening there.

I grew up in small spaces, with walls close by, hearing conversations in all rooms, no matter where I stood. Twenty steps from the front to the back of the house. A picket fence enclosed like a safety blanket for the family of six living together. I liked to sleep with the clothes dryer running--it was next to my bedroom --and the rhythmic thump thump put me to sleep. My bottom bunk bed provided a canopy of squeezed space. It was like being bundled up in a sleeping bag. And when taken out of that safety net of limited space, occupied with family noise, for an extended length of time, I, as a teenager, didn't know how to cope.

Second semester I turned eighteen, made friends, felt comfortable in classes, and overcame my fears. No more hair pulling. No more panic attacks. My anxiety passed, never to return. Stepping back into my daughter's dorm room, I adjusted that box of stationary and book of stamps one more time and grabbed her now empty bags and boxes which we would need to repack in the spring, for her trip back home. It was time to leave her to this new life.

When I at 17 said goodbye to my parents, I hung on, not wanting them to leave. When my daughter said good bye, she gave us a quick hug and a kiss, and with a little push, took off to look for that five foot ten girl to talk more about the toils of having long legs. She was thinking about things an 18-year old girl should be concerned with: friends, parties, and yes, classes, and not fearful about what- if scenarios as I once was.

Serpentine Seas © Cara Bovaird

Dewy crags beneath my feet become

Medusa's petrified victims,

And hint at the algid waters below.

I leap, but the fear lasts only a second.

Immersed, surrounded and

Numbed.

She hisses beneath me, and her

Emerald tresses caress my feet.

The icy womb of the serpentine sea cradles me.

She coaxes me deeper, yet

My mortal frame will not

Unleash me.

It is my sempiternal soul

That will remain below with the

Ophidian Goddess.

Violent splashes rise from the waves

As my body tries to emerge.

Sunlight is visible yet out of reach,

I grasp towards the surface.

But the serpent coils itself around an ankle

And at once the sunlight disappears.

Medusa, termagant, virago,

Witch.

Addiction © Chris Maxwell

groping still

for coping skills

that permanently alter pain.

too often the ticks

only complicate the tension

plunging me into a maze

of hostile design

and hidden doubt;

nailing me to the scaffold

of relentless pursuit

and restless poverty.

as endless debts accrue

i don't know what to do;

my cleverness perishes in a

demanding deluge of

alienation, consequences,

obligation and simulation.

masks cover hurt

only on the surface.

medication numbs affliction

only for a season:

a short season. a season

that melts into a reality of

greater grief and growing guilt.

within and without.

so close and so far.

victory and defeat.

i groan for redemption, for release.

can i live here?

will help arrive before it's too late?

Blackout © Hillesha O'Nan

We head towards the East...

To escape the chaos

The sky

Starless

Is thickened with darkness

With no cars passing through

Dare any light shine?

No longer human

They

THEM

Watching

Waiting

To pounce any innocent passerby

Flesh for flesh

There's nowhere to turn or hide

This is the blackout

© Hillesha O'Nan

Sleight of Hand © David L O'Nan

My blood is an old soul

That should be pumping through a robotic poet from classic times

If I'm breathing you will hear me

When I'm not, you may hear me more

How else can you see these supposed fast-moving clouds dream –

As slow motion tantras through a heartless sky?

This current world is too loud for me,

Yet it isn't nearly loud enough

The art is secluded

The arteries are clogged,

Filled with supernovas and suffering

And they call this a sleight of hand

Come Possess Me in the Rain © David L O'Nan

The conduits all say that I invented myth

And magic all in one breath.

There is a mist in the cold air

On a Greenwich Village Halloween night

I can not feel the electricity

Only the forceful druids, and the chanting wish of death

They hold me up and say

Come Possess me in the rain

Licks the cold steel to my skull

Possess me, with me

Real and muted by the shame

In an execution style parade

What is the impression of a concrete stain?

They are practicing Shakespeare

They are faux Warholas and Bohemians in sunglasses

Without a notion of care

And I'm in this shadow that you feel at the River

Cold to the touch, blood like paste

The arrows kill the stars in the nuclear waste

In the air, decaying the ground

Now I'm expected to love all

As I'm pierced to these skyscrapers

Bound and bullied

My hands shaking off frost

It takes every breath in my lungs to

Release all my cowardice and all the vapors

Like this militant view of my skewering

They drop me off like unused flesh

Love was only the invention

Off the roots of an untimely reptilian dream

And hate grew in the garden

And shook the city lights to the seas

There isn't a Picasso left

Digging up from the cracks

I crawl up through Cherry Lane

And I watch all the faints

And my nerves constantly dance an alarm

I am rushed in my steps

I am hushed in the slivers of my brain

In my mind that never sleeps

In my possession they fed off for years

I can only find truth and humanity

And live like I'm the Palomino

Dodging in and out of the hustling of fear

The Mystery of Mount Sterling © David L O'Nan

They washed the blood

From the rocks to the seas

A wall of towers

Crash to the ashes of banging drums

Still heard in rumbling hungers

Of Mount Sterling

In the orphanages, in the cries of lost land,

We can now march as the spark off the reenergized phantoms

Say goodbye in hallucinations

Where we saw Heaven in a viewmaster

In the distances, in the hint of the kingdom

But, when do we begin running towards the golden flash?

Captured me, erased me

Severed the ties of cultures and families

Washed me in the clots

And left me there a mystery

Waiting for the crows to connect the dots

Your Stare © David L O'Nan

I climbed out of your watch, your stare

And stopped time

To erase hours that leave me bare

To age defacing me

To the crippling of the bones

I will be resurrected as the spotted falling leaves.

Choked © Megha Sood

Your vapid thoughts

lodged in my throat

stuck between

the ashen dreams and the reality

like an illusion

a mirage,

like an impossibility of the summer rain

Your pungent thoughts

settled like arid leaves

with its stench carried

throughout my body

those capillaries of failed promises

like the bowl of milk left overnight

left to curdle

baring the stench of a failed ambition

a continuous struggle of my existence

I'm feverishly trying

to regurgitate these sullen thoughts of you

from my reticent mind and screaming soul

a moment sublime:

to breathe fully

to finally feel alive.

That Searing Pain © Megha Sood

How can a fleeting emotion

a mere mention of your name

or a visage bearing a semblance of yours

torments and rattles my soul

the searing pain hasn't stopped yet

the blood hasn't

chipped or dried yet

those memories

hasn't turned into a bookmark

a thing of the past

an affair to be forgotten

that smile

still not foreign to me

as the memory of

your warm embrace too

these old memories

with pointy and dagger precision

splits and shreds me to pieces

the pain comes flashing back

as I trample the

unburied consciousness of time

moments so precious

spent in the company of yours

It leaves me baffled

startled how much

a mere sense of your presence

can rattle me from within

aching from the core.

Cocoon of Misery © Ulane Vuorio

Some days

I am tight wound

like coiled spring

bundle of frayed nerves

just looking for escape

way to lash out

my frustration

I am wrapped

in black velvet

of endless night

closing around me

cocoon of misery

holding me

in rigid embrace

of my own mind

I feel like

time is running out

whichever way I turn

road is standing up

but I know deep down

there has to be

a way for life

to get better

Then the Day Came... © Raine Geoghegan

I remember your body lying in the darkened room,

the smell of stale air and socks.

How you had become ghostlike,

silent, creeping about the house.

I missed the boy in you, the joy in you.

In the afternoon you'd come downstairs,

go into the office where the computer sat.

You moved your fingers on the keyboard

at the speed of light as you played game after game,

not stopping to eat or drink.

There were two sides of you.

The quiet one, soft voice, sad face,

eyes filled with longing.

The other, set like stone, words forming sharp arrows,

wounding me, wounding you.

Then the day came,

when I felt the weight of all that you were holding onto,

and I wondered if you could hold on any longer.

On that day I kissed your forehead

as you lay in bed, the voice of Michael Jackson

on the radio singing Billie Jean.

A sharp memory of you aged five dancing,

shouting 'OOW.'

When I returned home late that night

and saw you in the kitchen, you were making scrambled eggs.

You were dressed, you were calm,

your eyes looking straight at me

and you said. 'Hi Mum, how did the workshop go?'

Seaside Towns © Iona Murphy

Time moves differently here. Everyone knows everyone and keeping secrets in a bottle is impossible, somehow, they always get thrown out to sea. Wherever you go he's always there. When you close your eyes his face floats amongst the static fuzz. When you open up your bedroom window in hope that the autumn rain tiptoes in, instead the scent of his aftershave wafts through and your room isn't safe anymore. He's there. He's there. When the home phone rings whilst you lay in bed you hear that voice reply back. It's his voice. It's always his voice. His lullaby pulling you under. Goodnight little one. Even when you're asleep you're still trapped in that dead-end town. Waves lapping at your ankles beckoning you further from the shore. Nothing around but darkness. You look to the moon but all that sits in the sky is his face. The omnipotent presence looming over every choice you make. His hand picks you up out of the waves, you're screaming, begging someone, anyone, to let you slip under the surface and never bob back up to the top. He laughs and his hand tightens around your upper arm. Your paper bones go up in flames from the lit stick of incense between his thumb and forefinger. Another night you can't escape. The past never stays where it belongs. Time moves differently here.

Coyote Song © Peach Delphine

Not yet dead already ash,

Already invisible, unknowable,

Smell the sea just beyond the pines,

Hear the wind combing out salt Marsh,

Osprey call, mullet get eaten,

Gather up what you can

We will flee with falling light, with coyote song,

Emptiness of waves welcome us, mangrove

Conceal our passing,

Not yet dead, already gone,

Sleep with one foot against the door,

It's your neighbors that will come for you,

After coffee, eggs and bacon,

What my father never knew,

The sharpest blade

Is for cutting sorrow.

Dark © Ivan Peledov

I am tired of midnight wasps

that can't stop counting the roadkill and

the horizons smothered by blabbering mountains.

The bones of cannibal ancestors have been cooling off

in the company of age-old suns. Sunflowers shudder in the dark.

84 (Any Scar) © Peach Delphine

Cutting was the secret language

of moon and moss

textured layers of shadow

without day or spark

oaks hold themselves penultimate

ancient in a landscape of erosion

cabbage palms shaggy

with my supplications

sheaves of paperwork

endless recitations of symptoms

a midden of discarded words

what we cast off

wave tumbled round

sea is my only certainty

liquid incandescence

saltier than blood

smoother than any scar

Curtain House Wounds © Foy Timms

At the bottom of these eyes, there is a quiet stirring

as streets wake up and mornings fall abruptly between us.

We were prising open a memory

with the blunt scissors of noon,

when our lone child leapt from these arms

across a season's unfaithfulness,

introducing a silence heavier than bone.

After Watching 'Behemoth' © Jack Bowman

Phosphorous, radium enlightenment
Uranium 238 smile,
the scientist from the NRC
watches the sky,
mystery crashes in the atmosphere

wonders in sci/fi;
'if aliens are changing the atmosphere so it's easier for them to breathe'

or if that's just another excuse for greedy, heartless sapiens
to pollute the planet

sad, acid, fog tears, burns, scars
Earth trembles

waits for another large asteroid,
already past due

or some new dangerous giant to come up from the ocean depths
to do a little payback.

Fall Coming © Jack Bowman

Movement from summer that bakes, tags along,

insomnia trials

very little sleep permitted, something in the air

contrails dropped by an invisible UFO over Chile'

 searching for answers, digging in, ancient sites,

carvings made out of jade, who knows when,

scratches on cave walls, lights in the sky

all come to a head

with no head

eventual disclosure polluted by conjecture

and an inability to do anything about it

accept

watch, take pictures, discuss, share, film,

make a plan that may never get executed

a gas that may not allow breathing.

Anima Lost in the Woods © Jack Bowman

Edgy pharmacologic experiments,

attempts to deal with isolation,

formation of pathways;

synaptic paths; dirt and mud, rocks, hazards

razor sharp weeds and large buzzing insects

 she withdraws into her own books,

word collections, multiple concepts of reality and

attempts to reach some answers

for pain

Why her?

Why do they tear at her?

She pours herself back into "Ariel" 'Anne Sexton' Poems

and quotes out loud, shattered pieces of 'Lady Lazarus'

her face is wet,

her heart angry

and her dreams are shadowy images from

Gothic and Italian horror films

she is only sure its 6:30pm

and

she exists.

Skeleton Trees © Kaitlyn Luckow

It's not like she didn't plan on coming here. In fact, if she was brave enough to be honest, a part of her yearned to be here. It all led up to this: home.

The forest, with its skeleton trees that still produced impenetrable shadows, made her feel as if this was where she belonged.

She looked down at her t-shirt that used to hug her chest, but she didn't need to be hugged anymore. This was no place for that. This was a place where all around you moved in. The trees enveloped you in their arms and held you as close to their ragged trunks and fallen leaves as they could.

She had been here before; the trees creaked to her and sang her a song that hallowed out her soul so that she could make it whole again.

The roots of the trees, the ribs of the trees, jutted out of the earth, but she didn't try to avoid them. She liked the twinge of the sharp points, liked the way the rough edges took her breath away so she could try to breathe again.

She looked around, desperately hoping to see her again. Last time, she had disappeared into the roses before she had a chance to finish. Not this time. This time would be different. This time, maybe the thorns would keep her.

The shadows of the skeletons wilted away to make room for the stars that never came. But she was still able to see. The only thing she needed to see was the dark.

A gust of wind overtook her entire body and she felt emptily whole as she smiled.

She was here.

She filled her lungs with the wind and breathed out ash. It danced in front of her like blood in water until the ash started to come together to create her pointed face of razor cheeks and jutted lips. Her black wings were her cloak that she bathed in and sparse feathers dotted her skull as the remaining ashes blew away.

Her black wings folded down over arms and she held out her hand.

"Give me your hand, Lily," the woman said.

Lily held out her hand and touched her finger to the woman's. Black ink started to fill up her hand with cold and the black danced around her wrist and rooted itself through her elbow.

The woman smiled down at her when it was filled.

"Welcome home."

The woman floated across the fallen leaves and wrapped her wings around Lily.

"My dear, I can finally wrap my wings all the way around you." The woman kissed her on her cheek. "And I can finally feel your bones."

Despite the wings, despite the kiss, Lily was cold.

"Don't be afraid, darling. It's okay to be cold."

She could always read her mind. That was Lily's favorite part. Someone understood. Someone made her not feel like, as her mother would say, "crazy".

"Being cold only means that you can feel." The woman smiled.

The woman lifted her wings and held Lily away so she could look at her.

Lily stared back. Hoping she wouldn't see. Hoping she wouldn't notice--

But the woman lifted her eyebrows knowingly. "Lily."

"I know," Lily whispered. "I'm sorry." She dropped her head to look at her thigh peeking out underneath her shirt. The skin bulged up, the lines a gross reminder of all of her mistakes.

The woman put her hand on Lily's thigh. "Let me help you."

The black ink flowed from her wings, through Lily's thigh. As the ink dripped from her body, so did the fat, so did the lines.

Lily felt relief.

"Thank you," Lily whispered to the woman.

But the woman didn't smile back, she didn't take away her hand. She only furrowed her brow. "It is not enough," she said in a flat voice.

Lily's eyes widened as she looked down at her legs to see them dripping, dripping, dripping with ink. A black pool filled the forest floor. But it just kept dripping. Her legs kept dripping. Disappearing. Lily looked back at the woman, panic filling her lungs.

"Please," Lily said.

"Not enough," the woman said flatly, not looking at her, but smirking at the pool of black she was creating.

Lily tried to move, but she was trapped. She couldn't lift her feet. And it kept dripping.

But then, she spotted it, a flash of red. A flash of thorns behind the woman who wouldn't stop.

The roses reached up like flames behind the woman and swiftly grabbed her by the by the wings. The force tore away her hands. The ink started to dry up.

"But, dear. We're not done yet. We're so close," the woman said calmly as the rose branches started to lift her up. Her eyes told of panic.

Lily didn't say anything, frozen to the forest floor amongst the ink.

The roses lifted up its branches and dug it's thorns into the woman's skull. The woman screeched as her feathers started to give way to ashes.

"Lily, you don't want this. You need to--"

The largest and brightest rose lifted its bulb over the woman's face. It opened up its petals and collapsed over her screams. The thorns disintegrated the darkness into mere ash, and all was silent.

Lily felt something warm slide down her hollow cheek. She lifted up her finger and wiped the tear across her face.

Maybe she didn't have to be hollow.

This forest never had to be her home.

The Hills of Almaden © JP Meador

I wish the houses on the hills

would disappear

With a wave of a hand

And the dish on Mount Umunhum

would return

Like to see the streaks of snow run

down the mountain

Once again in the winter

I was raised at the base of the hill

Where the orchards

and oaks were plenty

And the meadows were just

a step away

The color of the hills were bright green

and blue

And the fields were spotted

among the brush

(thinking of a brook) © JP Meador

A sound so tranquil

and comforting

Forging its own way

Through the landscape

The stream trickles down

flowing over the pebbles and rocks

as it moves down into a ravine into a pond

A large oak tree stands among

tall grass and wildflowers

Its branches stretch out

in all directions, pulling for the sky.

Places I Remember © JP Meador

The places I remember

growing up are now gone

or they don't seem important anymore

I like to think, it's only a phase

I'm going through

It feels like

I got my fill

For the day

The feelings stagger in

And out through the years

I wonder what this is telling me

Are they revealing?

Something

That is absent in me

Is it a tug on my shoulder?

Are you forgetting something?

Which always leads me back

I don't know if I belong here

Or somewhere over there

The memories I carry

Intensify this growing concern

Why should I worry?

I have no bearings

And I'm moving along

Using my senses as a guide

The Search © Joan McNerney

We are the lost who have

climbed hillsides...gathering

innumerable and unnamed

stumbling over sharp rocks

searching for our long shadows.

Tracing darkness with

vagrant fingertips

tasting the disdain of dust

we are long shadows

moaning with open mouths.

Eating bitter food grown

on the wrong side of this moon

our hearts caged in fear

fearing we have been cast off

fearing we have no destination.

Sands burning our feet

whipping our unnamed faces

we are long shadows crossing

this dessert longing for

an end to our thirst.

We are losing our shadows

entering empty caves

now listening for echoes

now finding wells of memories

innumerable and unnamed.

PTSD © Karen Mooney

Guilt, fear, anxiety, strangled by

restraint translates to anger

Blazing like full sun, falling in shame

hiding behind the covers of night

Piercing howls in moonlight

belie the charming macho front

Jovial, authoritative character

The strong silent type, he won't talk

Asks why you want to know

Resents his own body's ruthless

betrayal of his darkest secrets

yet he takes them out, on you

Broken © Karen Mooney

Broken

I found you this morning,

all folded up, tucked in

at the back of my mind's drawer

The one marked 'do not open'

Perhaps, it wasn't closed

tightly enough, over filled

contents ready to spill

if touched by hoping

You appeared in jewelry boxes

cards, photos, concert tickets;

in a souvenir mug that cannot be

held; its handle long since broken

Tree of Crows © Stephen Sherman

High up along the branches as some fruit in barren tree

the crows have gathered for a quorum sitting silently.

A twist of head the only motion that betrays some stir.

A twist of head, then stillness long, as other crows concur.

They seem like ordinance stocked up high on a shelf displayed

They seem a jury pondering with chin on palm arrayed

They seem to wait for bus or train to travel into night

and patient are those passengers, sun setting on their flight.

The crows they sit and gander at each other's inky mane,

the sun asetting crimson hues on branch, on crow as flame.

And lurch these large and on'rous things foreboding some avail, and as to where their trek will call one hopes to tell the tale.

All Souls Day Star © Stephen Sherman

A single Star on All Souls Day was brilliant in the night.

The darkness had consumed the sun

and grasped up all the light.

But there it shone just to the north as twinkles went to sleep.

Their eyes were drearily consumed

and awake they could not keep.

"What haughty brilliance brought to us?" the twinkles dreamt soon on.

Our eyes are wrestled with that shine

what "Souls Day Star" bought on.

But laughed away the "All Souls Star" that shined too bright to see,

for now that twinkles shine to sleep,

the "All Souls Star" shines free.

The Rustling of the Satin Dress © Stephen Sherman

The Beast that bodes accompanyment is silent by her side.

It offs a leer, it's head to sway nose down while plying by,

Not even steps are heard from Beast as Beast and breath collide

and colored doom as darkened room as saunter'd shoulders wye.

But why does Beast, like trusted friend ne'er fail to leave her side?

Her task must e'er be sure fulfilled without a singlest threat

and soleful role and arbiter to dispatch those implied

is Beast forever, Beast anon, and Beast whom Gods ne'er met.

Her fingers long and supple touch with gentlest of care.

Her eyes as deep as star filled nights seek those of last breath bound.

Her divine whisper "Come thee hence" as song from lips in aether,

her downey cheeks can bare no tears as wings angelic found.

Divine ever and tearless hostess to whom all life confess.

Ages keeping ear on guard for Rustling of her Satin Dress.

Hometown © Ann Hultberg

I left you for warmth, but I missed the feel of your chill, your imprints left on window panes and

scarf bundled faces. I left you for the squawk of the seagulls, but I missed the call of the turkey,

its rapid gurgling waking up the sunrise. I left you for navel orange trees, but I missed seeing the

star-shaped pink Mountain Laurel, a carpet for the forest glen. I left you for the scent of the sea,

but I missed your pungent smell, wafting throughout town, its heavy scent left on clothing.

I wanted to permanently leave you for glamour and skyscrapers, but I couldn't. I wanted to

ignore you, move out and never look back, but you wouldn't let me. I thought you were boring,

your facades never changed, and you were even ugly at times – scarred, pockmarked like a

ruffian from an old mobster movie. You cried incessantly and clouded the joys of a sunny day.

Yet, not until I left then returned did I realize your charm and what you had given me: salmon-

colored roses and magenta lilacs in summer and slopes to ski in winter; nighttime noises like the

pumping beat of the power houses on the hillsides and the train as it whistled through the valley.

You let me relax and meditate within the reds and oranges of the maple leaves, without any

hurry. You showed me shade under the weeping willows, as tall as they are wide, and fields of

soft-white Queen Anne's lace; finding cold streams filled with minnows and boulders large

enough to climb, I wandered off by myself, safely hidden among the hills, because you protected

me.

Some made fun of you. They thought they were classier, more refined. They had traveled and experienced worlds unknown to you. You were criticized and compared to what they had seen-- miles of seamless asphalt melting into the horizon, bright lights screaming for attention, bustling congestion flowing on every sidewalk--but they offered no way to make you better. But maybe you are fine the way you are: old and small and slow paced in a modern world-- that is your appeal. And though many have left you, the new ones have discovered your secrets:

Milk cows lumbering across the road, from field to barn,

Chirping crickets, bedded in the dewy grass, looking for mates,

Spotted fawns nibbling at the hundreds of crab apples dripping down from trees,

Sacred silence, at the summit of a cemetery, overlooking the broccoli tips of forest trees grooming the sky, exudes the presence of a higher power.

You are the secret garden, ours to enjoy, naturally.

And though your name is not on my birth certificate, I think of you as mine.

Leda and the Swan © Rumillenial Poetry

Startled! Shocked! Oh, poorest bird.

Beating wings of ecstasy.

Cries of bugles that I heard

Flew for life, it came for me.

Thighs on thighs, caressing soft

Nape and back of neck in bill

Unconsenting senses loft

Mounds of soft on feathered fill

Shake and tremble, hands are numb

Cannot push thy glorious self

Loosen body, thighs succumb

This whole acts turning me helf!

Rush inside, pulsating deep

Heart beat's stranger where it lies

Taking over, raging seeps

Insides turn. A strange disguise.

Am I dreaming? Did I see

Death destruction all around?

Broken wall and widows weep,

Agamemnon dead! Lay on ground.

Such illusion! Boding future.

No free will! Can't make it stop.

Indifferent unlikely suitor

Feathers twitch! That beak did drop.

Violent sky, I held my breath

Overtook body and soul

Infinite and not with death,

God of Gods just made me whole...

Spinning Dreams © Niles Reddick

Nita loved going to school and wanted to be a writer. At night in her shared room with

sisters Kate and Louise, she wrote poems and stories she heard from others about the Native

Americans, about her brother Jack who was killed in the WWII, and ghost stories. About sixteen,

She'd met a boy who wore glasses and who buck danced at a barn sing and was cheered on by

his three sisters. Jacob called on Nita and they shared an orange on the front porch of Nita's family's farm, a white clapboard house constructed in a pecan grove for shade and flanked by cotton fields in which they all worked.

After a few dates, Jacob and Nita told him she'd have to talk to her parents. She really Didn't want to marry Jacob, or anyone, but wanted to go on to college with her friend Madeline and be a writer. That night, she shared her journal with her parents, spun her dreams for them and shared Jacob's proposal. They didn't care for Jacob because he was even poorer than they were. Nita's mother snatched the journal, flung it into the fireplace, said she'd marry Jacob and move out, doing so would be one less mouth to feed, and Nita ran to her room and slammed the door. Her daddy spit tobacco juice into a spittoon, and her mother went to the kitchen, sat in front of the fan that kept her from sweating so much when her sugar ran high from the garden corn.

"You should've told them over breakfast. You know how Mama gets at night with her high sugar," Kate said.

"Think I ought to bring it up again in the morning?" Nita asked.

"Once she's made up her mind, its over just like a storm pushing through. It does what it does and moves on," said Louise.

"What about your notebook?" asked Kate.

"Burned completely," Nita said. "But its up here." She tapped her forehead.

Within the month, Nita's mother had bleached an old cotton dress for a ceremony in the yard by a circuit preacher, and Jacob and Nita took a horse and buggy through the woods to his Uncle Joe's unpainted house with a dirt yard. They ate barbecued pig and sipped corn liquor until they went to bed. Jacob climbed on top of Nita. She felt some discomfort and tickling sensations until Jacob rolled off sweating and out of breath.

Months later, Jacob worked at the dairy, milking cows. Nita kept the rented one bedroom house clean and suckled the next generation to her breast. She vowed the girl would have a different life than she had and the previous generations of women in her family, but the dreams spun in minds dissipate with time and another generation comes, goes, and rationalizes their lives were better ones. The dreams are taken away by the breezes that come and go.

Lilacs © Jackie Chou

Dad's voice in my ears,

After all these years,

 Lilacs the color of dreams,

Reality starker than it seems.

The callouses on his hands,

Evidence of life's demands.

Too blind to see the truth,

He thought I had it smooth,

Not knowing what lay ahead

The road on which he tread.

The fallen lilacs only covered

The hardships I discovered.

(blue ink) On Interviewing with Abercrombie and Fitch © Jennifer Criss

You don't know,

but I saw what you scrawled

at the top of my resume

in big, bold letters

Too fat

All caps

Blue ink

Underlined twice

You didn't ask

about my experience,

my degrees,

or my values.

You'd already made up

your mind the minute you

saw my frumpy skirt

bought to impress you

Too fat

All caps

Blue ink

Underlined twice

I'm sorry, that I only

look good on paper

and not in person.

Not the right face, right body.

I'm not sure you heard

a word I said

about my work ethic

and my life goals

Too fat

All caps

Blue ink

Underlined twice

I'm growing tired

of doing twice

as much to prove

I'm half as good.

I have value,

albeit in a bigger package,

but I am worthy

no matter what

you write down.

Too fat

All caps

Blue ink

Underlined twice

Finding Music in the Every Day © Jennifer Criss

I hear the orchestra of the rusted screen door

screeching open and shut and open again.

The percussion of raindrops on the roof above

lull me into a sleepy trance.

The hum of the metal fans work hard to move

the stifling summer air.

The chorus of the crickets' song seeps through

the windows and into dreams.

The band of laughter swells from the kitchen table

through the hallways and under doors.

And this is the music of my everyday.

This is the song of home.

For as Long as I Remain © Linda Crate

when i think of home

i imagine house

of my parents,

they live in a place with

an ageless face

whose beauty sighs in clouds

and blue skies and trees tall as

skyscrapers;

it is in the fields and forests i spent

a lot of time growing up—

the loner no one understood

unraveled herself in thick puffs of white clouds,

endless blue skies,

choruses of rambling creeks and babbling brooks,

in fields of orange wild lilies growing by the side

of the road,

in the wings of butterflies and crows;

there is peace to be found in the heart of this place

so i focus on those memories when i can

because not every memory is potatoes and gravy

some are heavy stones i try to chisel away—

but in nature i found pieces of me

that music and books couldn't give,

and a peace that will cleanse me for as

long as i remain.

You're Always There © Linda Crate

when i remember home

it is inevitable

that i remember you

i wish sometimes

the rain could wash away

past memories,

but you are in my recollection;

in my bones

haunting me over and over—

when will it ever be

enough for you?

you hunger for something

that was never yours,

and i told you no;

but you tried to take it anyway—

then at college,

when i was finally loosening my petals,

beginning to feel safe

you found me;

"i bet you don't remember me", you grinned

all i could do was stare like a doe

caught in the headlights

of a vehicle

gutted by a ruthless hunter

hungry for blood

no matter the cost—

why couldn't you leave me alone?

the forced kisses i insisted

you didn't take,

the attempted rape;

now when someone tells me

i have a pretty smile it's a trigger

and you are shooting over me

over and over again

until all i want to do is crawl

into the bones of a past self so you

cannot torment the current me—

it never works,

you're always there.

This Place Isn't Mine © Linda Crate

i miss living in the town i grew up in, home cooked meals and dusty dirt roads; a village

of trees and stalks of corn taller than me—there were always adventures to be had in the

woods, always secrets the wind would tell me; i would always uncover some new

mythology of my name and bones—i miss being able to wake up to a sunrise and see a

sunset clearly, where the hustle of city life wasn't so predominant; a place where i didn't

feel threatened simply by existing—i miss the moments spent in tranquil nature, listening

to crowsong and dancing beneath the moon; visits to the beach or standing in the creek,

hearing the psalms of trees—i don't like this place of endless sidewalks, buildings, and

the omnipresent arrival and departure of vehicles; i like the music of the country better:

the mooing cows, the cawing crow, the songbirds, the barking dogs, and singing crickets; everything is better than the constant beeping and whirring of people focused on being somewhere other than where they are—i just want to wrap myself up until i can be husked and boiled away from this place and come out shimmering, new, beautiful, and reformed.

Anxious © Cee Martinez

tears at the bottom of every attic in my heart slip through the cracks

the puddle in my belly

never dries

I wear scrapes on my scalp

and my skin doesn't help

to protect when the worry is inside

drive

me to my sailor

drive me from my jailor

and I say I'm too stupid to drive

i depend on depend

and your willingness to spend

and anxiety drains this fount

bare me if you can

and I'll bear your withstand

and both of our backs will break

Redecorated ©Richard Waring

my old bedroom

childhood's stronghold

papered over and repainted

near the carpet's edge

a jutting nail

and underneath, the floorboard

the hidey-hole

the secret place

where treasure and shame

were hidden

reaching inside that hollow space

its contents gone

discovered and removed

decayed or turned to dust

Upon Waking © Richard Waring

I remember ice

inside my bedroom window

even my breath did not melt it

a single pane of glass

rattling in the wind

colder outside than in

but only just

Tell Me the Truth (Not About Love or God) ©Matt Duggan

Tell me the truth –

Not about LOVE or GOD

rain will change colour

inside wet and warm circles

I'd see the reflection – of every lover

past and present;

Tell me the truth about YOU

let us throw a penny

into a draining stream

watch a river rise over

the snubbed and decayed

where the anti – sapiosexualist

spins one hundred million voices

that sound the same -

same treadmill winds on

They roll them up – Spit them out

Please tell me the truth

(Not about Love or God)

before too many ego's

spoil this imperfect broth.

Beware of a God that Smells of Liquor © Matt Duggan

Beware of a God that smells of liquor

he'll change the route and imply the simplest of distractions

while sipping gin with cucumber (not lime)

whisper to the ocean to break our mast

among a thirsty crew that create masks;

across tables where chameleons

sleep with tanned and bitten feet;

Feast on Caldo Verde and cold sardines

clinking of wine glasses,

the slaughtered lambs are easily replenished;

pretentious permanence hangs in the hot air

where we hear nine different dialects

trying to delete the madness from the remains of day.

Weavers of tapestry point out our fates

around capes and sunken shipwrecks

gleaming under surface like opened pots of honey

shining and paused underneath in blue and turquoise green.

Make it to the island where eyes are full with rain

guide us to a vertical wind far beyond

the touch of a drunken god's watery grasp

we shall rise as the tellers of journey, birth, and past.

The River Only Flows West When the Dead are Sleeping © Matt Duggan

Guilty sentiments

stored in cupboards

where birds –

no longer wake us with song;

If I ever see the stars

breathing out again

that majesty of light

that hangs like shining chariots –

carrying angels

across yellow moons;

I will gaze -from the corners of east and west

when our past is caught

in a clock's mechanism -

metal boats in industrial blue

sleep beneath feet

resting oyster catchers will glimpse

ends of passing

dream and waking breath

the river only flows west

when the dead are sleeping.

© Hillesha O'Nan

Overexposing Us © Scott Christopher Beebe

he says "it's time for me to go"

this had been during the gloaming

remember the one?

it'd sparked a world controversy

not over wrong or right

color scheme, nothing so

daunting as that kind of plight

instead, it'd been over

ancient crucibles that

bore more truth

in the aphotic

funny how I mention this -

so flip, it drips in clips & sips

when I'm breathless over the mess

we'd made of this

- us -

this thing we'd given

far too much attention

"what are your intentions?"

he asks me, like it's

about measuring

dimensions

when it's gauged

by dark & cold

or so we'd been

overexposed

I don't know how

to answer him

or myself,

for that matter

I'd not known

there'd been anything

about which to question

At the Movies © Scott Christopher Beebe

We splurge on popcorn at the movies, though this food has

to last us exactly one week. Feed our greedy gullets on it, obtain

a refill from the concession counter - keep ourselves from gorging

on it for this has to last us til payday. Tuck the bag beneath the

seats at our feet. Wag our digits along one another. Search his

profile awhile instead of the film unveiling its story to us.

Audience laughs & cries out at appropriate places. His face is all

the entertainment I need to feel satiated.

Thrills layer up on top of chills that spill over and fill me up.

It's a good thing, as I'm no longer hungry for the week's

sustenance which he gets to eat until we receive our checks. On

the way home, he holds it in one arm, and me under the other.

After so many years together, it's his spell in which I'd not once

minded dwelling.

host of these harmless procedures © Scott Christopher Beebe

the game's always this same shaming thing - ignites a light,

making me feel high inside; sense of trouble has doubled

beneath the rubble of stubble his whiskers & liquors have

discovered a way to make me obtain a world of pain from

evolution's proof in sustaining the plague that's bottled up in

gumdrops or something equally non-harming, which is good

because I'm disarmed by how unalarmed I am at how his charm

is harming to me - it'll be the end of me; stay til then & you'll see

BIOS:

JOHN EVEREX: I started inventing stories as a child and haven't stopped.
I write on Twitter (@EverexJohn) and publish work regularly on my blog
(http://johneverex.blog) as well as through chanillo.com
My writing comes in various forms and lengths, including microfiction, flash fiction and short
stories. I also write poetry, being especially fond of haiku. Currently, I am working on a new
novel, which will be published in 2020.
In addition to writing, I am a father, husband and teacher and currently live in the south of
England

ANN HULTBERG: Ann Hultberg is a retired high school English teacher and
currently a composition instructor at the local university. Her degrees are in
English and reading education and educational psychology. She writes nonfiction
stories about her family, especially focusing on her father's escape from
Budapest, Hungary, to the United States.

Twitter is Ann Hajdu Hultberg@ Hajdu This fall three of her essays will be
published in *Drunk Monkeys*, *Persimmon Tree*, and *Dream Well Writing*.

CARA BOVAIRD: Cara Bovaird is a English literature Masters student from Donegal, Ireland.
She enjoys spending time by the sea and both reading and writing poetry. She is also known
as the resident Sylvia Plath fanatic to her university classmates.

CHRIS MAXWELL: Chris Maxwell served as lead pastor for 19 years and has worked as
Director of Spiritual Life at Emmanuel College for the last 13 years. He speaks around the
worldin churches, conventions, and epilepsy events. He has written nine books, including

Underwater – his story about epilepsy – and his most recent book, a slow and sudden God: 40
years of wonder.

www.chrismaxwell.me

HILLESHA O'NAN: Co-Editor of Fevers of the Mind Poetry Digest/Fevers of the Mind Press. Has her own blog covering fashion, motherhood, travel since 2004. Can be found on Instagram under @Hillesha

DAVID L O'NAN: Editor of Fevers of the Mind Poetry Digest, has been writing and performing poetry, prose, short stories since 2003. Currently has a book nearly 500 pages collecting poetry written between 2003-July 2019 "Reflections" available on Amazon Paperback & Kindle. He has also put out an Anthology book "Avalanches in Poetry" available on Amazon Paperback & Kindle which is a book of inspired writings by contributors who were influenced by Leonard Cohen. Can be found on FB writer page DavidLONan1 Twitter: @DavidLONan1 @fevers of for the litmag page. A best of the net nominee.

MEGHA SOOD: Megha Sood lives in Jersey City, New Jersey. She is a contributing editor at Free Verse Revolution, Heretics, Lovers and Madmen, Sudden Denouement, Whisper and the Roar, GoDogGoCafe and Poetry editor at Ariel Chart. Over 300+ works in journals including Better than Starbucks, FIVE:2: ONE, KOAN, Kissing Dynamite, Mojave Heart Review, Adelaide, Foliate Oak. Visitant Lit, Quail Bell, Dime show review, etc. and works featured/upcoming in 20 other print anthologies by the US, Australian, and Canadian Press. Two-time State-level winner of the NAMI (National Alliance on Mental Illness) NJ Poetry Contest 2018/2019.National level poetry finalist in Poetry Matters Prize 2019. She blogs at https://meghasworldsite.wordpress.com/ and tweets at @meghasood16. Instagram: @meghasworld16

ULANE VUORIO: Ülane Vuorio is a poetess and amateur photographer who finds inspiration spending time outdoors in her beautiful homeland of Finland. Her passion is nature and macro photography, finding beauty in small things that often go unnoticed. Ülane started reading and writing at age five. Books and words still at the center of her life today. Working as a freelance interpreter made her fall in love with versality of words. She enjoys flash fiction and dreams of publishing her own book of poetry and photography. You can find her on Twitter at @UlaneVuorio

RAINE GEOGHEGAN: Raine Geoghegan, MA, is half Romany and lives in Herefordshire in the UK. She is a Pushcart Prize, Best of the Net 2018 and a Forward Prize nominee. Her work has been published both online and in print with Poetry Ireland Review; Under the Radar; The Travellers' Times; The Ofi Press; Romany Routes and many more. Her work has been featured in documentary films. She gives reading in the UK and Ireland. You can follow her on Twitter.

IONA MURPHY: Iona Murphy is an English Literature Master of Research student at The University of St Andrews. She is a feminist, bisexual, mental health advocate, and spends most of her time engrossed in the works of Sylvia Plath. She has poetry published in Black Bough's 'Lux aeterna' collection, Teen Belle's 'Catharsis' anthology, 3 Moon's 'One Six One Nine' anthology, and The Fruit Tree's 'Joy' issue. She has creative non-fiction published with Ayaskala, Ang(st) Zine, Brave Voices, and Mid-Heaven Magazine. You can keep up with her on Twitter @write_with_iona and Instagram @ionasmurfy

PEACH DELPHINE: Cook, animal person, obsessed with the mangrove forest and barrier islands. Can be found on Twitter @ Peach Delphine from Tampa, FL

IVAN PELEDOV: *Ivan Peledov lives in Colorado. He loves to travel and to forget the places he has visited. He has been published in Eunoia Review, Thirteen Myna Birds, Unlikely Stories, Illuminations and other magazines.*

https://www.facebook.com/ivan.peledov

FOY TIMMS: Foy Timms is a poet based in Reading, Berkshire, U.K. Her work has been published or is forthcoming in Glove, Hypnopomp, North of Oxford, Peeking Cat Poetry and Pulp Poets Press, among others. She is preoccupied with themes such as departure, solitude, British towns/villages, social exclusion and the sociopolitical dimensions of living spaces. Twitter: @FoyTimms

KAREN MOONEY: Karen has been scribbling lyrics and poetry since 2016. Her work has been published in USA, UK and Ireland. Publications include Vox Poetica, Hedgehog Poetry Press, I am not a silent poet, Poetry 24 and former cactus.

Facebook: @observationsbykaren
Twitter: @1karenmooney

JOAN MCNERNEY: *Joan McNerney's poetry has been included in numerous literary magazines such as Seven Circle Press, Dinner with the Muse, Poet Warriors, Blueline, and Halcyon Days. Four Bright Hills Press Anthologies, several Poppy Road Review Journals, and numerous Kind of A Hurricane Press Publications have accepted her work. Her latest title,* The Muse In Miniature, *is available on Amazon and she has four Best of the Net nominations.*

JACK BOWMAN: Rock, Blues, Art and Spoken Word.

Jack G. Bowman is a Licensed Psychotherapist (LMFT MFC42855) Poet, Composer, Artist and Performer in Southern California. His poems have been widely published in small presses across the US, UK, India, Mexico and on the internet since 1991. He has written reviews for Poetix and Poetic Diversity, he was a member of the poetry groups; Third Person Singular, Duotribe and The Furniture Guild Poets, in recent years, he has been published in Altadena Poetry Quarterly and Spectrum Anthologies, He was nominated for a Push-Cart Prize in 2016.

Jack G Bowman MA LMFT 42855

1. http://www.youtube.com/JackGBowman

2. http://www.facebook.com/jackgbowman

3. https://www.goodreads.com/jackgbowman
4. http://www.amazon.com/-/e/B00F5DJ6TI
5. http://deviantart.com/jackgbowman

6. all books available at Http://www.Amazon.com or http://www.thebookpatch.com/SiteSearch.aspx?q=Jack%20G.%20Bowman

   original music also available on www.cdbaby.com &

http://www.Amazon.com see

KAITLYN LUCKOW: Kaitlyn is a writer based in Portland, OR. Her roots are in education and she was a high-school English teacher for five years before taking the leap to follow her passion for increasing compassion and understanding through storytelling in writing.

She believes in the ability of writing as a vehicle for empathy. In order to tell stories that unite, she believes in the power of well-crafted writing, honest storytelling, and creating stories that connect.

Her creative writing has been previously published at Wide Eyes Publishing, Barren Magazine, and The Crybaby Club.

https://www.kaitlynluckow.com

https://twitter.com/kaitlynluckow

https://www.instagram.com/kaitlyn.luckow/

JP MEADOR: JP Meador is the author of twenty -five books of poetry and five Novellas, including Passing Through and Moore's Story. He lives in Fresno with his wife Debbie and their grandson Matthew.

https://www.amazon.com/Not-What-You-Think-Collection-ebook/dp/B07V4VPXQJ/ref=sr_1_3?keywords=not+what+you+think+jp+meador&qid=1566919696&s=gateway&sr=8-3

STEPHEN SHERMAN: Stephen Sherman was born on the birthday of Walt Whitman. He lives in the Coney Island area of

Brooklyn. Stephen Sherman has been writing most of his life including hundreds of poems and several albums of copywritten music. He has been involved in acting, professional singing, production of a video Blog hosted by famed journalist Bill Weinberg and is presently coming to the retirement of a career as a Civil Service Supervisor. For decades he has been a proponent of progressive agendas, civil and woman's rights. Sherman has interests in Hindustani and Carnatic music and dance and Eastern Philosophy.

"Do your work, do it well, have fun doing it."

RUMILLENIAL POETRY: Born in the late October of 1985, Zickey Marya, aka Rumillenial poetry, is a man who became a writer by chance. A Physical Therapist by profession, he was not into the poetry circle up until mid-2016. One fine day, while fixing something electrical, he got an electric shock which seems to have scrambled his brain. Since then, he hasn't stopped writing. A lover of the universe, he writes about love, loss, mental health, dark poems about sadness or despair and nature. His heart is always with the words, trying to write another heartfelt piece. His poetic root could be found in the great poet Rumi, however, Zickey wanted to go a different route to find the light in this book, through the darkness.

2) Twitter handle: *@rumillenial*

3) Instagram and Facebook handle: *@RumillenialPoetry*

4) Previous books, features in other books and anthologies:
   a) Glad To Be Mad (my debut book) Available on Kindle and Amazon.
   b) Ambient Heights (A Collective Anthology) Available on Amazon and Kindle.
   c) Dangerous Elysium (By Author Natalie Serna) Available on Amazon and Kindle.

NILES REDDICK: Niles Reddick is author of the novel *Drifting too far from the Shore*, two collections *Reading the Coffee Grounds* and *Road Kill Art and Other Oddities*, and a novella *Lead Me Home*. His work has been featured in eleven collections and in over two hundred literary magazines all over the world including *The Saturday Evening Post, PIF, New Reader Magazine, Forth Magazine, Cheap Pop, With Painted Words,* among many others.

Website: http://nilesreddick.com/
Twitter: @niles_reddick
Facebook: https://www.facebook.com/niles.reddick.9

JACKIE CHOU: Jackie Chou writes free verses, rhyming poems, and Japanese short form poetry. Her work has been published in JOMP 21 Dear Mr. President anthology, Creative Talents Unleashed anthologies, LUMMOX, and others. She was nominated for a Best of the Net in 2017 by Hidden Constellations.

JENNIFER CRISS: Jennifer Criss graduated from Ball State University with minors in Creative Writing and Criminal Justice. She writes mostly short stories, but has recently discovered a love for poetry. Her work has been published in *Poebita, Whispers, The Poet Community, Indiana Voice Journal,* and in several print anthologies. She was nominated for a Pushcart Prize in 2016.

LINDA CRATE: Linda M. Crate's poetry, short stories, articles, and reviews have been published in a myriad of magazines both online and in print. She has six published chapbooks *A Mermaid Crashing Into Dawn* (Fowlpox Press - June 2013), *Less Than A Man* (The Camel Saloon - January 2014), *If Tomorrow Never Comes* (Scars Publications, August 2016), *My Wings Were Made to Fly* (Flutter Press, September 2017), *splintered with terror* (Scars Publications, January 2018), *more than bone music* (Clare Songbirds Publishing, March 2019), and one micro-chapbook *Heaven Instead* (Origami Poems Project, May 2018). She is also the author of the novel *Phoenix Tears* (Czykmate Productions, June 2018).

CEE MARTINEZ: Cee Martinez is an artist and writer from Colorado, USA. She has struggled with ADHD and depression her entire life but takes solace with writing and painting. Her poems and short stories have appeared in numerous online and print magazines and she was nominated for a 2012 Pushcart Prize for her work in "Short, Fast, and Deadly".

RICHARD WARING: Richard's work has appeared in the 2019 CAP anthology and Black Bough Broadsheets issue 1.

MATT DUGGAN: Matt was born in Bristol 1971 and now lives in Newport, Wales with his partner Kelly his poems have appeared in many journals such as *The Potomac Review, Foxtrot Uniform, Dodging the Rain, Here Comes Everyone, Osiris Poetry Journal, The Blue Nib, The Poetry Village, The Journal, The Dawntreader, The High Window, The Ghost City Review, L' Ephemere Review, Ink, Sweat, and Tears, Confluence, Marble Poetry Magazine, Polarity, Lakeview International Literary Journal,* Matt won the *Erbacce Prize* for Poetry in 2015 with his first full collection of poems *Dystopia 38.10* and became one of five core members at *Erbacce-Press,* where Matt interviews poets for the *erbacce-journal,* organises events and reads with the other members for the annual erbacce prize.

In 2017 Matt won the *Into the Void Poetry Prize* with his poem *Elegy for Magdalene,* and read his work across the east – coast of the U.S.A. with readings at the prestigious Cambridge Public Library Poetry Series in Boston, a guest poet appearance at The Parkside Lounge and Sip This in New York City, Matt read at his first U.S. book launch in Philadelphia and has two new chapbooks available *One Million Tiny Cuts (Clare Song Birds Publishing House)* and *A Season in Another World (Thirty West Publishing House)* plus a small limited edition booklet *The Feeding* (Rum Do Press) Venice and London. Matt was also one of the winners of the *Naji Naaman Literary Honours Prize (2019)* and has read his work across the world including The Poetry on the Lake Festival in Orta, Italy, at the Poetry Café in London, A Casa dos Poetas in Portugal, in New York, Boston, and Paxos in Greece, and various venues across the U.K. His second full collection *Woodworm* was published by Hedgehog Poetry Press in 2019.

SCOTT CHRISTOPHER BEEBE: Scott Christopher Beebe has authored 20 books for his publishing imprint Steering 23 Publications. All are available for purchase on Amazon. He created the hashtag #ConverStory on Twitter in April, 2019 which has writers create pieces with a daily word he provides by utilizing only conversation. His poetry and stories have been published by the first three editions of Fevers of the Mind Poetry Digest, along with poems "Jailbait 8" and "divorcing Eve" for PENMEN REVIEW from University of Southern New Hampshire in the fall of 2019. He can be followed on Twitter @storysmithscb where he daily participates in writing prompts #vss365, #TransWrite, #BraveWrte and #microprompt.

© Hillesha O'Nan

COPYRIGHT PAGE:

Printed in the United States of America in Evansville, Indiana

First Printing: November 2019
Amazon ISBN: 9781688815513

Imprint: Independently Published

Printed by Amazon Italia Logistica S.r.l.
Torrazza Piemonte (TO), Italy

10303209R00045